THe
"I NeeD
HeLP
NOW"

ALSO KNOWN
AS THE **STUDY**
"I SHOULD HAVE
DONE THIS **COMPANION**
WEEKS AGO
AND DIDN'T" **AUTHORED BY**
GUIDE TO **Jennifer HOYER**
SUCCESS **AUTHORED WITH BOB HOYER**

ISBN: 1482391155

ISBN 13: 9781482391152

TABLE OF CONTENTS

Foreword

It is a special honor and privilege to be asked to prepare the Foreword to I Need Help Now. What makes this book timely is the accumulating body of evidence demonstrating the profound importance of executive skills and learning strategies in promoting school success in youngsters. Indeed, a voluminous body of research has documented the deficits in learning strategies/executive skills in students diagnosed with ADHD and learning disabilities. However, students without disabilities often lack these skills as well, and can certainly benefit from the strategies in this text.

Particularly noteworthy in this book, is the inclusion of concrete, specific, and detailed steps students need to undertake to be successful in school. These techniques can be easily adopted by parents, educators, counselors, psychologists and even the youngsters themselves.

Authors Bob and Jennifer Hoyer are experts who draw upon over twenty years of experience in the field of education. In fact, as a practicing Child and Adolescent Psychologist who conducts psycho educational evaluations, it has often been a relief to me to be able to refer clients to the Hoyers because I know they will help youngsters be academically successful. I congratulate the authors for an informative and hands on text and trust the reader will find it as practical as I have.

Jack Cramer, Ph.D.
Licensed Psychologist
Private Practice
Roswell, GA

INTRODUCTION

THIS BOOK IS BASED ON THE IDEA THAT STUDY-SKILLS BOOKS ARE NOT THE BEST PLACE TO LEARN STUDY SKILLS.

This is so true that I will skip the lengthy introduction, the long discussion of left brain and right brain, cognitive influences, and the painstaking process of questionnaires and interviews to help you decide how your child learns. Really, if you think about it, your child already knows how he learns best. He loves flash cards or hates them; she is great at taking notes or prefers to listen; he will read his textbook or he won't. The problem is, despite your constant begging, she lacks the maturity and discipline to take the extra thirty minutes required every day to review notes, read texts, and memorize information.

As a result, your child shows up for tests unprepared.

This book is written to fix that. This book will be a companion to your child—a friend he can turn to and find techniques and worksheets to use in that moment to help him complete a project, prepare for a test, or even write a paper.

Author's note:

This book does not need to be completed in order. *Your child should look for the chapter title that seems to solve his problem for the moment and proceed from there.* After each chapter, there is a follow up chapter that explains how to deal with the lack of preparation before the next test. Some children appreciate the input and naturally take the advice. Others need to be required to read and apply this information and submit their "study tasks" daily. This is your opportunity to get as involved as you need to be in building success for your child. You may notice some repetition among the chapters. This is not an error. Because I can't predict which chapters a given student will need, I wanted to ensure that every chapter contains every relevant detail. Since there are similar approaches in subjects like social studies and science, you may notice some overlap if you are working in both subjects.

For the purpose of simplicity the student in this book will be referred to as "he" and the teacher will be referred to as "she". Nothing is intended or implied by this choice it simply makes the book easier to read.

If you're interested in how these techniques were developed or would like information about the people and years of experience involved in putting this book together, please visit academicsolutionsga.com.

For now, there is studying to do..

PART I

IS THIS GOING TO BE ON OUR TEST?

Notes, texts, novels, and other such struggles

I Have a Test Soon, and My Notes are Terrible

Okay, so you have a test and your notes are terrible. Yes, your parents were correct: you should have been taking better notes all along. (We will talk about that in chapter 1-A). But you didn't, so what next? Well, you will need your textbook and a pen, preferably one that is a different color from whatever you took your terrible notes with in the first place.

Go get those things and meet me back here.

First, you have to realize that this is going to take some time and effort—right now. *But don't give up!*

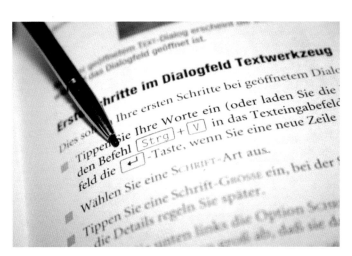

Instead, let the aggravation you feel at having to do this all right now fuel your fire for doing it in advance next time.

Second, you have to determine how you will be tested.

I am assuming you opened this chapter because you have a class that is mostly "note driven." So this section is designed to teach you how to study for a test in a class that can be at least partially described by one of the following:

1. My teacher doesn't use the book.

2. My teacher makes her own tests.

3. My teacher's lectures don't include everything we need to know for the test.

First let us clear up a few classic misunderstandings.

☐ The fact that your teacher doesn't use the book should in no way suggest that *you* are not to use the book.

◇ What your teacher is really saying is that the class (and therefore the test) is largely driven by the notes given in class. However, you can rest assured that your teacher is not making up the information in your science or social studies class. She has certainly used the text as a guide for what will be discussed in class.

◊ That said, unless you have perfect listening skills and exceptional note-taking skills, the only way to achieve a better-than-average grade in the class is for *you to use the book*. The following steps will help organize the way you should use your textbook in a class like this one.

HERE IS WHAT YOU WILL DO FOR RIGHT NOW:

STEP ONE: Put together all the notes you have for this test, so they follow the order presented in your textbook.

STEP TWO: Read the portions of the chapter that match up with the notes your teacher gave you. As you read, fill in your notes with information from the chapter that improves upon what you wrote down in class. If you think about *what* you are writing down as you write, you won't have to spend as much time rereading all of this at the end. (Yes, that means off with the computer, the phone, the ear buds, and the TV.)

STEP THREE: Read through your notes and, as you do, make a test for yourself that includes the questions you think your teacher will ask you on your real test. Your test should include the following:

☐ A list of terms and definitions; consider if your teacher usually has you fill in the blank or match definitions with terms

☐ Any diagrams that you will need to either label or explain

☐ A number of fill in the blank questions that pull together the main points discussed in class or in the text

☐ Any potential essay questions that tie together ideas discussed during this unit of study

Remember, the more difficult and complete you make this test, the more likely you are to do well on the real one. Challenge yourself at this point, and success will be yours!

STEP FOUR: Compare your test to the tests in the back of the chapters you have been studying in your textbook, then add anything to your test that the text includes but you did not. Now go back and make sure that you have this new information in your notes as well.

STEP FIVE: Take a break that is anywhere from five minutes to two hours, depending on whether the test is tomorrow (five minutes) or in the next couple of days (two hours).

STEP SIX: Attempt to take the test you made for yourself. Take it like it is the real thing, with no breaks and no peeking at the chapter or your notes.

STEP SEVEN: Grade your test. Go back and make flash cards of everything you missed. Now review some more until you are ready.

LAST STEP: Make a vow that you will not wait until the last minute ever, ever again. Get some rest and do your best on the test.

After school tomorrow, come back and read over the next chapter (1-A)to learn how to prepare in twenty minutes a day and be totally ready before the next test without any of the stress you just experienced. Make plans to read it tomorrow, or this is sure to happen to you again.

Reminder: You may notice some repetition in the next chapter. That is because chapter 1 is a shorter version of chapter 1-A. That's ok, take your time and soak it in, Chapter 1-A is how you are supposed to study and it is much easier than what you just did!

THE "NEXT TIME" SOLUTION
FOR STUDENT WHO STRUGGLE
WITH NOTE TAKING

This section of your study-skills program will teach you how to prepare for a class that can be at least partially described by one of the following statements:

☐ My teacher doesn't use the textbook.

☐ My teacher makes her own tests.

☐ My teacher's lectures don't include everything we need to know for the test.

☐ My notes are not very good.

First let's review the classic misunderstandings that may have put you into this position in the first place.

☐ The fact that your teacher doesn't use the textbook should in no way suggest that *you* are not to use the textbook.

◇ What your teacher is really saying is that the class (and therefore the test) is largely driven by the notes given in class. However, you can rest assured that your teacher is not making up the information in your science or social studies class. She has certainly used the text as a guide for what will be discussed in class.

◇ That said, unless you have perfect listening skills and exceptional note-taking skills, the only way to achieve a better-than-average grade in the class is for *you to use the textbook*. The following tasks will help organize the way you should use your text in a class like this one.

◇ For this to be easy and work properly, you simply need to promise that you will complete one task each day from the minute your teacher introduces the new chapter until the night before the test.

HUGE POINT: You don't study for a test. You study because there *will eventually be* a test. You have two choices: get ahead and succeed, or stay behind and risk failing. If you are reading this section, you have made the best choice and are ready to succeed.

While the following tasks are organized in a logical order, you do not need to work in that order for this process to succeed. If your teacher starts the lesson with a discussion of a graph or diagram, try the diagram task(Task 4). If she starts with a lecture, use the "Notes to text" task (Task 1). Find the tasks that help you grasp the information the best. Eventually you should find that you have completed them all anyway, so order doesn't matter.

TASK 1: FROM CLASS NOTES TO TEXT

Take your notes from class and, using the text, reread the chapter as you fill in information that improves your notes and makes them clearer for you. Attach this page with a paper clip to those notes. Remember, your teacher makes her own tests, so lead with her notes but make sure you use the text book to ensure they contain all of the information you might need for the test. Do this one section at a time and follow up after each section with task 2.

TASK 2: SECTION REVIEW

After you have rewritten your notes from one section, answer the questions in the section review in the space below without using your notes or the textbook. Then investigate anything you can't answer: Did I not have it in my notes? Did I have it in my notes but not think it was important? Add information to or highlight your notes so you will remember these key things.

Answers to the section review:

Chapter: _____ Section: _____

Answers to the section review:

Chapter: _____ Section: _____

Answers to the section review:

Chapter: _____ Section: _____

Answers to the section review:

Chapter: _____ Section: _____

TASK 3: TERMS FOR A HISTORY TEST

While there a many ways to study vocabulary, most students just memorize definitions. This works fine for a few words, but what if the words are historical terms, such as *Enlightenment* and *Scientific Revolution*, that actually contain ideas, people, and theories about what people believed? To study this type of vocabulary, you will need a plan. Always remember that if you just memorize the words, you will be fine for the test, but if you *learn* the words, you will be set for the rest.

Organize the words to be studied under a logical topic. For example, study all the words related to types of government (*dictatorship, anarchy, monarchy*). Then group the words that deal with branches within the government (*legislative, bicameral, judiciary*). This will help you focus on fewer ideas. It is easier to think about four groups of words than it is to memorize forty individual words.

TASK 3A: TERMS FOR A SCIENCE TEST

While there are many ways to study vocabulary, most students just memorize definitions. This works fine for a few words, but what if the terms are scientific and include a process (*digestion* or *mitosis*) or diagram (plant cell) that you will have to understand? For this type of vocabulary, you need a plan. Always remember that if you just memorize the words you will be fine for the test, but if you *learn* the words you will be set for the rest.

Take the words to be studied and organize them according to a topic. For example, study all the words related to digestion together, and then group the words related to the function of the heart and so on. This will help you focus on fewer ideas. It's easier to think about four groups of words then it is to memorize forty individual words.

TASK 3A AND 3B: MAKE FLASH CARDS

Cut out these squares and make flash cards of the terms in the section.

TASK 4: COPY THE DIAGRAM(S)

Copy the diagram(s) in the space provided that contain(s) important information for your test. Make a quiz for yourself out of the diagrams, charts, or graphs in the chapter.

Diagram: _____ from page _____

Quiz questions:

1.

2.

3.

4.

5.

Diagram: _____ from page _____

Quiz questions:

1.

2.

3.

4.

5.

TASK 5: MAKE A TEST FOR YOURSELF

Using your improved notes, flash cards and diagrams, make a test for yourself. This test should include ten questions from each section and any terms that are still unfamiliar to you. This should go beyond the section review quizzes you made as you rewrote your notes and include harder questions that you think you might not remember for the test. Compare the test you made with the chapter review and assessment in your text book. What did you miss? Did you have some questions that were far too simple than the ones asked by the author of your textbook?

Add any questions you overlooked to the test you made. Then you will have a great study guide.

Chapter: _____ Section: _____

1.

2.

3.

4.

5.

6.

7.

8.

9.

10.

Chapter: _____ Section: _____

1.

2.

3.

4.

5.

6.

7.

8.

9.

10.

Chapter: _____ Section: _____

1.

2.

3.

4.

5.

6.

7.

8.

9.

10.

Chapter: _____ **Section:** _____

1.

2.

3.

4.

5.

6.

7.

8.

9.

10.

TASK 6: TAKE THE TEST

TASK 7: TAKE THE TEXT BOOK'S CHAPTER ASSESSMENT AS A TEST

Don't use your notes or your book as you do this.

Check yourself. Identify what you still don't know, and study that information more thoroughly.

List your answers to the chapter assessment test below:

- _____

  _____

- _____

  _____

- _____

  _____

- _____

  _____

- _____

  _____

- _____

  _____

- _____

  _____

- _____

  _____

CHAPTER 2

MY Teacher Lectures In Class and Then Gives us a Test That Has nothing to do with Her Lecture

When you experience this in a class it is usually for one or both of the following reasons:

◊ Your teacher uses premade tests that are produced by the publisher of the textbook, and as a result you feel like the notes given in class are not related to the test you end up taking

◊ Your teacher has a tendency to get off the subject, and you tend to get distracted and miss information as a result.

The key thing to recognize is that this is actually *fantastic!* You have a teacher who is giving you a test that was written by the same exact people who wrote your textbook. This is superb! All you have to do is learn how to read a textbook thoroughly and use the tools in your textbook to prepare for your test. In this case, your teacher's lecture serves mostly to keep you interested in the material and to point out the most important parts of the text.

The second thing to realize is you cannot cram under these circumstances, which is why there is not a chapter 2-A named "I have a test over eighty pages of text tomorrow and I haven't started." Textbooks are painfully thorough, and you will have to digest the information in chunks or you will never remember it all. Tasks 1–7 will be the most useful to you in this class. If you do have a test tomorrow, choose the most relevant tasks in this chapter and get busy! After your test, read the entire chapter to ensure you can prepare for your next test ahead of time.

TASK 1: READ AND OUTLINE THE SECTION

As you outline focus on the information that is most likely to be on a test over this chapter. If you include too few details you won't be ready. Include too many and you will have too much extra information to deal with in the end. Complete one section at a time and follow it up with Task 2 to make sure you have included the right information.

Helpful hint: if you struggle with note taking in class, bring your completed outline to class and simply *add* information that your teacher mentions that is not already written in your outline. Remember, she is not making up this stuff; she studied the textbook and is explaining it to you. Follow along and improve your outline as she lectures.

Begin below and attach the extra pages you use.

Chapter: _____ Section _____

I.

    A.

    B.

TASK 2: SECTION REVIEW

Use your outline to answer the questions in the section review. Use only your outline. Investigate anything you can't answer by asking these questions: Did I not have the information in my outline? Did I have it in my outline but didn't think it was important? Add information to or highlight your outline so you will remember these key things.

Answers to the section review: (Each chapter and section needs a full page)

Chapter: _____ Section: _____

1.

TASK 3A: TERMS FOR A HISTORY TEST

While there are many ways to study vocabulary, most students just memorize definitions. This works fine for a few words, but what if the words are historical terms, such as *Enlightenment* and *Scientific Revolution*, that actually contain ideas, people, and theories about what people believed? For this type of vocabulary, you will need a plan. Always remember that if you just memorize the words, you will be fine for the test, but if you *learn* the words, you will be set for the rest.

Organize the words to be studied under a topic. For example, study all the words related to types of government (*dictatorship, anarchy, monarchy*). Then group the words that deal with branches within the government (*legislative, bicameral, judiciary*). This will help you focus on fewer ideas. It is easier to think about four groups of words than it is to memorize forty individual words.

TASK 3B: TERMS FOR A SCIENCE TEST

While there are many ways to study vocabulary, most students just memorize definitions. This works fine for a few words, but what if the terms are scientific and include a process (*digestion* or *mitosis*) or diagram (plant cell) that you will have to understand? For this type of vocabulary, you need a plan. Always remember that if you just memorize the words you will be fine for the test, but if you *learn* the words you will be set for the rest.

Organize the words to be studied under a topic. For example, study all the words related to digestion together, and then group the words related to the function of the heart and so on. This will help you focus on fewer ideas. It's easier to think about four groups of words then it is to memorize four individual words.

TASK 3A AND 3B: MAKE FLASH CARDS

Cut out these squares and make flash cards of the terms in the section.

TASK 4: COPY THE DIAGRAM(S)

In the space below, copy diagrams that contain important information for your test. Make a quiz for yourself out of the diagrams, charts, or graphs in the chapter.

Diagram: _____ from page _____

Quiz questions:

1.

2.

3.

4.

5.

Diagram: _____ from page _____

Quiz questions:

1.

2.

3.

4.

5.

TASK 5-6: MAKE A TEST FOR YOURSELF

This test should include ten questions from each section and any terms that are still unfamiliar to you. Compare the test you made with the chapter review and assessment in the text book. What did you miss? Did you have some questions that were far too simple than the ones asked?

Add any questions you overlooked in the test you made. Then you'll have a great study guide for yourself.

Chapter: _____ **Section:** _____

1.

2.

3.

4.

5.

6.

7.

8.

9.

10.

Chapter: _____ Section: _____

1.

2.

3.

4.

5.

6.

7.

8.

9.

10.

Chapter: _____ Section: _____

1.

2.

3.

4.

5.

6.

7.

8.

9.

10.

Chapter: _____ **Section:** _____

1.

2.

3.

4.

5.

6.

7.

8.

9.

10.

TASK 6: TAKE THE TEST

TASK 7: TAKE THE CHAPTER ASSESSMENT IN THE TEXT BOOK AS A TEST

Don't use your notes or your book as you do this. Then check yourself. Identify what you still don't know, and study that information more thoroughly.

List answers to chapter assessment below:

- _____

  _____

- _____

  _____

- _____

  _____

- _____

  _____

- _____

  _____

- _____

  _____

- _____

  _____

- _____

  _____

TASK 7: CLASS NOTES

Make sure your notes from class have all been accounted for in your outline, flashcards, and diagrams from tasks 1-6. Double check to ensure that your teacher didn't mention anything in her notes that you overlooked in studying the chapter. After you have added in anything from her notes to your outline, your study packet is complete!

CHAPTER 3

I Have a Test on a Novel/Short Story That I Didn't Understand

THE "RIGHT NOW" SOLUTION

Well, you are in a bind, aren't you? The best thing you can do for yourself *right now* is to use all of the notes, worksheets, and study guides that your teacher has handed out to help you reconstruct what happened in the story If the story is short enough to reread, certainly begin there. If not, follow the steps below for a short-term solution.

To avoid this situation in the future, make a promise to yourself to use chapter 4 from the beginning the next time a reading assignment is given.

STEP 1: Assemble all the materials and notes you have on the story.

STEP 2: Use these notes and the story to complete "Task 3: Literature study sheet." This sheet will help you organize the key components of the story and provide a basic grasp of the story line.

STEP 3: Know your characters. Use the "Task 4: Character analysis worksheet" to isolate the key people in your book and their significance to the story.

STEP 4: Be able to summarize the conflict. Very few teachers will let you off the hook if you aren't able to explain the conflict around which the story is built and how that conflict is resolved. Spend extra time on this step; you won't regret it.

STEP 5: Understand the words. Learn any words you didn't understand as you read the story. Pay particular attention to literary terms learned in class (*consonance, symbolism, irony,* and so on.) "Task 5: Important vocabulary" can help you isolate these.

* YOU WILL NOTICE THAT TASKS 1 AND 2 ARE NOT USED HERE... THOSE ARE TOOLS FOR YOU TO LEARN IN CHAPTER 4 AS YOU LEARN HOW TO STUDY A BOOK AS YOU READ IT.

TASK 3: LITERATURE STUDY SHEET

Title _____ Genre: _____

Setting (time, place):

_____

_____

_____

Theme (purpose, moral lesson, main point):

_____

_____

_____

Plot (the struggle, conflict, complications, and suspense in the story):

_____

_____

_____

_____

_____

_____

Climax (the point of greatest suspense; the turning point):

_____

_____

_____

Resolution (how the conflict is resolved):

_____

_____

_____

TASK 4: CHARACTER ANALYSIS WORKSHEET

Name	Description	Significance to story line	Key interactions

TASK 5: IMPORTANT VOCABULARY

Word	Definition	Example (include page number from story for reference)

CHAPTER 4

MYTH: YOU CAN'T STUDY FOR A TEST ON A BOOK; YOU JUST HAVE TO READ THE BOOK AND HOPE FOR THE BEST

If you're reading this chapter, you've probably tried to "just read the book and hope for the best" and realized it doesn't work. Novels, short stories, and poems can and should be studied, just like science, social studies, and math. (Yes, math can be studied. See chapter 5 for proof!)

The key to studying a story is to digest and analyze as you read so that (1) the story makes more sense as you read it, and (2) you are ready to prepare for the test as soon as you finish the book. Two birds...one stone!

The following tasks will help you organize your time so you aren't trying to read too much at one time. They will also help you break the book apart as you read for better understanding and synthesize the ideas presented once you have finished the story..

TASK 1: MAKE A READING PLAN

This is simple. Divide the total number of pages by the total number of days you need to read the book. Remember that you have to allow for time at the end to prepare for the test (or the paper you must write), so don't include those as reading days. Also consider that there may be a day or two that you can't read because your schedule doesn't allow for it. Subtract those days from the total number of days.

The number you get is how many pages you must read each day. Make a commitment to stick to that number, and you won't have to try to play catch-up at the end.

_____Days I have to finish the book/_____The total number of pages = _____Pages I must read each day

TASK 2: WRITE CHAPTER SUMMARIES

After each reading period, allow five minutes to take notes on what you have read. Do this immediately after you finish, and it will really help solidify your understanding of what you just read. Wait until tomorrow, and you will probably have to reread the chapter, which is a waste of time. Do it now; it won't take long.

KEY POINT: Do a good job. It only takes a few extra seconds to take complete notes, and this will save you precious hours the night before the test.

Use this chapter summary worksheet to summarize chapters.

Title _____

Chapter summary for chapter # _____

Main character(s) introduced (name and describe):

- _____
  _____

- _____
  _____

- _____
  _____

- _____
  _____

Key facts to remember from this chapter:

- _____
  _____

- _____
  _____

- _____
  _____

- _____

- _____

- _____

- _____

- _____

- _____

TASK 3: LITERATURE STUDY SHEET

Title _____ Genre: _____

Setting (time, place):

_____

_____

_____

Theme (purpose, moral lesson, main point):

_____

_____

_____

Plot (the struggle, conflict, complications, and suspense in the story):

_____

_____

_____

_____

_____

_____

Climax (the point of greatest suspense; the turning point):

_____

_____

_____

Resolution (how the conflict is resolved):

_____

_____

_____

TASK 4: CHARACTER ANALYSIS WORKSHEET

Name	Description	Significance to story line	Key interactions

TASK 5: IMPORTANT VOCABULARY

Word	Definition	Example (include page number from story for reference)

PART II

YOU EITHER KNOW IT OR YOU DON'T

Memory techniques and myths about studying

SO MANY WORDS, SO LITTLE TIME! QUICK FIXES FOR TOMORROW'S VOCABULARY TEST

Like many students, you probably figured you could wait until the night before and just cram all the words into your head and hold on to them long enough to spit them back out on the test in the morning. If you are reading this chapter, you have realized that there are too many words or the definitions are too difficult for that approach.

Before you get started on this chapter, make this promise: "I will study for vocabulary by looking at the words for ten minutes each day. I will read chapter 5 of this text tomorrow, and I promise to learn the words for a lifetime, not study them for one day." Once you have made that promise, continue on to learn how to solve your immediate problem. You will notice that only tasks 1 and 4 are discussed below. Tasks 2 and 3 are only useful when preparing in advance.

THE "RIGHT NOW" SOLUTION

TASK 1: Like it or not, at this point, flash cards are your primary option. And how you make the cards is critical. For a simple matching test, putting the word on the front and its definition on the back will work out just fine. But, if you need to know not only the definition of a word but also at least one antonym, one synonym, and the part of speech of the word, then your flash cards must look like this:

(Front)	(Back)
Word Part of speech	Definition: 2 antonyms (one you know, one you don't) 2 synonyms (one you know, one you don't)

Review these cards over and over. As you improve, separate the cards into two stacks: one with those you know instantly and one with those you need to practice.

TASK 4: Make a second stack of flash cards with just the words on the front. Spread both this stack of just words and the stack with the definitions on the back all over a table so you see the words and the definitions.

Now start a timer and time yourself to see how long it takes you to line up all the word cards with their definitions. Complete this task several times, each time trying to beat your previous speed. The faster you get, the more confident you will become as you commit the words to memory.

Remember, this is a short-cut. Unless you continue to work with these words, in a few days you won't remember a thing. To keep that from happening, start the day after the test with your new words and a long look at chapter 5-A.

THE RIGHT WAY TO STUDY FOR A VOCABULARY TEST: Ten minutes a Day and the words are yours Forever

Vocabulary is like addition. It's one of those fundamental skills that, once you learn it properly, is a blessing forever. Likewise, a weak vocabulary, like an inability to add numbers quickly, will haunt you for the rest of your life.

First, find ten minutes in each day that you regularly have available. You can tack it onto homework time, but you don't have to. Perhaps there is time when you are waiting for a ride to school, waiting for dinner to be ready, waiting for your brother or sister to get out of the shower. It doesn't matter when it is, as long as it is a regular daily time set aside for vocabulary.

Second, always have your stack of flash cards with you.

Choose any of the following tasks as a way to work with these words each day until they become a part of your natural vocabulary. Yes, you will eventually have a test on the words, and with this approach you will ace it easily, but more importantly, you will know these words forever.

TASK 1: MAKE FLASH CARDS

A well-made flash card solves many problems. When you need to know not only the definition but also at least one antonym, one synonym, and the part of speech of the word, your flash cards must look like this:

(Front)	(Back)
Word Part of speech	Definition: 2 antonyms (one you know, one you don't) 2 synonyms (one you know, one you don't)

Review these cards over and over. As you improve, separate the cards into two stacks: one with those you know instantly and one with those you need to practice. Obviously, if you do not need to learn antonyms and synonyms you can leave those off.

TASK 2: CREATE A SENTENCE

For each word, write a sentence that suggests the meaning of the word with context clues. Below are a good and a bad example of such a sentence.

Word: *elude*—to avoid cleverly (v.)

Good sentence: The boy _____ his captor by slipping away down the alley and into an open doorway.

Bad sentence: I _____ him.

The first sentence suggests the word is *eluded*, because of the key words *captor* and *slipping away*.

The second sentence is not good, because almost any word would fit and make sense (*kicked*, *liked*, *carried*).

By creating context clues that suggest the meaning of the word, you are training your brain to use those clues to find the meaning of the word as well.

TASK 3: CHOOSE YOUR FAVORITES

As you study the words and write sentences, identify five or six words that you could actually see yourself using—maybe not in daily speech with your friends ("Hey, guys, did you see how I eluded that bully at the party last night?"), but perhaps in an English paper that is coming due. Drop several words of this caliber into a paper and you will find yourself with a better grade.

Once you really know the information on these five or six flash cards, hole punch them and put them on a key ring or bulletin board so that the next time you write a paper or paragraph, they are available to help punch up your word choice. There is certainly a difference between "The main guy in the book got caught" and "The main character, unable to elude certain capture, decided to surrender."

TASK 4: DO SPEED DRILLS

As with anything, your speed and accuracy with a task is proof of your confidence. So once you have a strong grasp of the words, time yourself to see how quickly you can match the words with definitions.

You should already have the flash cards made up, but for this activity you will make a second stack of flash cards with just the words on the front. Spread both this stack of just the words and the stack with the definitions all over a table so you can see the words and the definitions all at the same time.

Now, time yourself to see how long it takes you to line up all the word cards with their definitions. Complete this task several times, each time trying to beat your previous speed. The faster you get, the more confident you will become as you commit the words to memory.

CHAPTER 6

MYTH: Everyone Knows You Can't Study For a Math Test

My first question here is, "What is your grade in math?" If you haven't been studying for math tests and you have a solid A, then good for you! You must be naturally gifted in math. If, however, you don't understand why you don't have an A, it is almost certainly because you think you shouldn't study for a math test.

Furthermore, if you are reading this the night before a test, I'm guessing that your grade is suffering a bit and this next test is an important one for you. As usual, make the promise: "I will learn to study for math tests at the beginning of my next lesson."

Now read what you have to do to get ready.

THE "RIGHT NOW" SOLUTION

Well, because you haven't been studying all along, you have quite a bit to do. The following checklist is meant to spread out your work over a week or two. Your job is to work through as many of these tasks as you can in the time you have left. Take your time. Try to think about the concepts and apply them until you feel confident in each one.

MATH TASK LIST

_____I have tried different examples in the chapter or from my handouts.

☐ Do they make sense to you? _____

☐ Can you do other similar problems? _____

☐ If not, ask a teacher/tutor/parent to go over the examples with you.

_____I have made flash cards of the highlighted and underlined words in my text book, handouts or class notes.

_____For extra practice, I have completed all the additional problems I could find in my worksheets, text book or related internet websites. If all the problems have been assigned, I have gone back and tried them again.

_____I have started a worksheet that contains new formulas I must learn, and I have reviewed them.

_____I have completed the short quizzes or section reviews in my book.

_____I have quizzed myself on the concepts in the chapter summary and from my class notes.

_____I have completed one or two of the *basic skills* (decimals, fractions, and so on) reviews that I found in the back of my book or from an internet resource.

_____I have identified the problems I am comfortable with and have worked on them with a timer to improve my speed so that on the test I can save more time for the problems that will challenge me.

TRUTH: YOU CAN AND SHOULD STUDY FOR A MATH TEST, AND YOU SHOULD DO IT EVERY DAY

For most people, doing math homework helps solidify what was learned in class that day. But frequently, that isn't enough. More often than not, to become a good math student, you have to *know what you are doing*. I don't mean that you can follow an example well enough to complete the even-numbered problems correctly. I mean that you understand the concept well enough that even if the teacher throws a curve at you, you'll catch it. Yes, even if that curve ball shows up in a word problem!

So, at the end of your homework each night, complete one of the tasks listed below. It will take only an extra five or ten minutes, but these are minutes spent really learning the concepts, which is exponentially more valuable than trying to memorize a process that you don't understand.

Keep this checklist with your notes from the chapter, and check off each task as you complete it. After a few chapters, you will probably start to develop some favorites from the list that really help you. Good! Make these a part of your regular study time, and watch your grasp of math grow.

MATH TASK LIST

_____ I have tried different examples in the chapter or from my handouts.

☐ Do they make sense to you? _____

☐ Can you do other similar problems? _____

☐ If not, ask a teacher/tutor/parent to go over the examples with you.

_____ I have made flash cards of the highlighted and underlined words in my notes, handouts or text book.

_____ For extra practice, I have completed all the additional problems I could find in my worksheets, text book or related internet websites. If all the problems have been assigned, I have gone back and tried them again.

_____ I have started a worksheet that contains new formulas I must learn, and I have reviewed them.

_____ I have completed the short quizzes or section reviews in my book.

_____ I have quizzed myself on the concepts in the chapter summary and from my class notes.

_____ I have completed one or two of the *basic skills* (decimals, fractions, and so on) reviews that I found in the back of my book or from an internet resource.

_____ I have identified the problems I am comfortable with and have worked on them with a timer to improve my speed so that on the test I can save more time for the problems that will challenge me.

Spanish is impossible!

Well, technically speaking, Spanish isn't really impossible. Many people learn the language quite well. Now, learning Spanish overnight? *That's* impossible. You probably don't remember this, but it took you four or five years from your first *mama* to create sentences that made sense to anyone. So give yourself a break, and remember: this is going to take some time.

As far as the test you have tomorrow, you will have to spend a lot of time memorizing the specifics of what you need to know. The tasks below will help with that. You will notice they are the same tasks used in chapter 7-A, but the difference is that tonight you have to do them over and over so you can pass your test.

Ideally, you would work these tasks regularly over time so you can absorb the language permanently. As far as the future of you learning Spanish, that will take a commitment of twenty minutes a day and a belief that, like millions of other people in history, you *can* learn a language. Chapter 7-A will help with that process.

TASK 1: SPANISH VOCABULARY 1

Make flash cards of all words. Put the Spanish word on the front and its English translation on the back. Add a memory cue to the front or the back to help you get started.

Quiz yourself on the words.

TASK 2: SPANISH VOCABULARY 2

Choose five words each time to write sentences—*in Spanish.* Yes, this seems hard, but the sentences don't have to be complex for this to work. For example, if the word is *vestido* (dress), you could write,

Es una vestido verde. It is a green dress.

Plus, this approach will let you use the verbs in the tense you are supposed to know, as well.

TASK 3: CONJUGATION PRACTICE

Fill out the grid below for each tense you are studying. Write a sentence with each form of the conjugated verb.

Verb: _____

Yo	Nos
Tu	Vos
El	Ellos

1. _____

2. _____

3. _____

4. _____

5. _____

6. _____

TASK 4: WORKSHEET PRACTICE

Take the worksheets you have been given in class, white out the answers, and copy the worksheets two or three times. Now try to complete the worksheets over and over until you get them right. Use your original as the answer key.

I am ready to Learn the Language

Good for you! Twenty minutes a day and the language is yours. The key things to focus on are vocabulary and conjugations. With those two areas mastered, you can make sentences, translate readings, and eventually carry on a conversation.

Read over the following tasks, and after you finish your homework for Spanish each night, take a few extra minutes to work on these. If you're behind in the class, a few catch-up sessions on the weekend will make a big difference.

If your lack of understanding goes beyond just putting in the time and work and you really don't understand how conjugations work or what the tenses mean, you need to see your teacher for an explanation of those concepts. But usually learning a language is about putting in the time and figuring it out.

TASK 1: SPANISH VOCABULARY 1

While there are many ways to study vocabulary, most students just memorize definitions. This works fine for some tests, but what if there are many words to learn? Or what if you need to put the word into a correctly translated sentence? The following technique will help you organize the words so you can *learn them* more quickly with less time spent on just memorizing.

Make flash cards of all words. Put the Spanish word on the front and its English translation on the back. Add a memory cue to the front or the back to help you get started. For example the word *vest* is *vestido*, which is also a piece of clothing.

Quiz yourself on the words.

TASK 2: SPANISH VOCABULARY 2

Choose five words each time to write sentences—*in Spanish.* Yes, this seems hard, but the sentences don't have to be complex for this to work. For example, if the word is *vestido* (dress), you could write,

Es una vestido verde. It is a green dress.

Plus, this approach will let you use the verbs in the tense you are supposed to know, as well.

TASK 3: CONJUGATION PRACTICE

Fill out the grid below for each tense you are studying. Write a sentence with each form of the conjugated verb.

Verb: _____

Yo	Nos
Tu	Vos
El	Ellos

1. _____

2. _____

3. _____

4. _____

5. _____

6. _____

TASK 4: WORKSHEET PRACTICE

Take the worksheets you have been given in class, white out the answers, and copy the worksheets two or three times. Now try to complete the worksheets over and over until you get it right. Use your original as the answer key.

PART III

THE Management OF TIME, TALENT, and TEENS

How to find your stuff and manage your time while not losing your mind

CHAPTER 8

STUDENT SECTION: WHERE'S MY STUFF?

First, you have to be honest with yourself—really and truly honest. Which of the following two scenarios describes you?

> I am really trying my very best to keep up with homework assignments, papers, and projects, but I can't come up with a system that always works.

OR

> I don't like doing homework. I don't want to spend my afternoons doing more school stuff, plus I don't feel like it helps anyway. Because of these feelings, I don't put much value in it, and so I forget to bring it home. Sometimes when I am made to do the homework, I don't bother to bring it back in. I just don't really care about it that much.

If you chose the second option, you really should take this page to your parents and share with them how you feel. You *need* to be honest with them too and discuss this issue. I promise you, it will not solve itself, and without a change, you risk falling so far behind that the help you eventually decide to get won't be enough.

If you chose the first option, read the following strategies that suggest a new approach to keep up with your papers and stay organized.

WHERE DOES IT HAPPEN?

First you have to figure out the moment at which you lose your stuff.

THE MOST COMMON PROBLEM: Teachers, eager to get in as much as possible, lecture right up to the bell. Then, as everyone stuffs books and papers into any opening they can find, the teacher begins to tell the class what is due the next day. And ,instead of listening, you were moving your feet into position to make the mad dash to the next class (allowing at least a minute to catch a friend or two in the hall, I'm sure). So, there is the teacher calling out assignments, and there you are stuffing papers into any place they will go. As a result, you end up at home without your assignment written down, and with your papers stuffed in all the wrong folders.

THE SOLUTION: Keep one thin folder with clasps down the middle and pockets on the side with you at all times. Keep one single sheet of paper in the clasps on this paper, jot down the assignments for each class for that day. When you walk *into* class, put it on the desk or right at your feet; it should always be within reach.

In the left pocket, put the things that must be turned in for the day, and in the right pocket, put the papers, handouts, and worksheets that must be completed that night.

One thin notebook with you at all times—keep it out, keep it handy, and put *only* your daily assignments in it. At the end of the day, stand at your locker and glance at the single page to decide which books you need; the homework/handouts should already be in the right hand pocket where you put them after each class.

KEEP IT SIMPLE

AT HOME: As you complete the homework, move it from the right side to the left side. Each night when you finish your homework, your folder should have an empty left side and a full right side. A quick check proves you have done your homework. Likewise, by the end of each school day, the right side should be empty, because everything should have been turned in. This very simple system gives you a quick visual reminder in each class of how you are managing your homework.

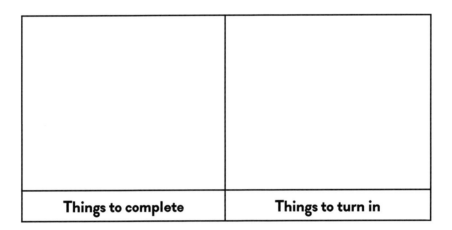

Things to complete	Things to turn in

There are a million other ways to manage homework. Truly, the best system is a simple one you can execute consistently and easily. If you think about it honestly, any system can work—if you want it to.

HERE IS THE *KEY*: To identify, finish, and turn in your homework, you have to make it a priority. Decide that you will do it, and do it. It really is that simple.

Parent perspective: WHY can't my CHILD FIND HIS STUFF?

Help for the chronically disorganized and/or motivationally challenged child

A college business professor could not help but notice that one of his students was late to class for the third time that week. Before class ended, he went around the room asking students some questions about the day's lecture. Of course, he made sure to pick on his tardy pupil.

"And who was it that developed the theories behind communism?" the professor asked.

"I don't know," the student said.

"Perhaps if you came to class on time, Mr. Reebs, you would know," said the professor.

"That's not true," the student replied. "I never pay attention anyway!"

AS A PARENT, YOU HAVE TO TAKE A SERIOUS LOOK AT YOUR CHILD AND DECIDE IF HE IS REALLY TRYING AND CAN'T SEEM TO MANAGE THE WORK LOAD, OR IF HE JUST DOESN'T PLACE AS MUCH VALUE ON DOING HIS BEST WORK AS YOU DO.

Before you try to solve this problem, you must honestly evaluate your child's situation. Try to answer these questions truthfully:

Does your child like to learn?	Yes	No
Does your child try his hardest on school work?	Yes	No
Is your child interested in academic subjects?	Yes	No
Does your child really care about his grades?	Yes	No

If your answers were mostly no, spending a lot of time trying to reorganize your child's binders, restructuring the time spent on homework, and helping your child memorize information for a test will not change the fact that he simply doesn't care about his school work as much as you do. This is a hard fact to accept, but once you decide that this is the case, you can move forward with a solution that can help him succeed.

Unfortunately, it's very difficult to make someone care about something. If a person hates snakes, for example, then handing her a snake, explaining how cute the snake is, and spending time convincing her how great snakes really are is not likely to change her opinion. She may eventually agree with you, but usually this is so that you will stop bothering her and take the snake away; then she can go back to hating snakes as usual.

Apply this example to your child's circumstance. How many times have you exacted a promise toward more effort, better grades, and stronger interest in school? How long has that promise lasted? Exactly. If you have not been able to convince your child of the importance of school so far (Plan A), you need to move to plan B or plan C.

If you are willing to let your child learn a very difficult lesson that will have a significant consequence, try plan B. If you are unwilling to let your child barely scrape by and want to insist that he succeeds, try Plan C.

PLAN B: ANTI-MANAGEMENT

This approach will take a strong will. If you're considering this plan, then up to this point it is likely that you have cared much more about your child's success than he has. This has to stop.

Believe it or not, when you show your child that you care more about school than he does, you send the message that he doesn't have to care, because you will make sure he succeeds. This is very similar to wondering why your child continues to leave his socks on the floor, even though you go by and pick them up every day. You may complain bitterly, but if you pick up the socks, wash, dry, and return them to the drawer each time, the real message is that it is okay to throw them on the floor.

So, it is time to let go. Take a deep breath, let it out, and decide that—pass or fail—your child will pay the consequences for not doing what he is supposed to do.

Make your expectations clear and the consequences very real. For example, you may believe that a reasonable effort from your child should produce all Bs on the next report card. Then tell him that you are no longer going to be involved in the academics of his life, that the entire process is up to him, *but* that if he doesn't get all Bs for any reason whatsoever, there will be a serious consequence.

This consequence has to be something you can and are willing to implement. You will also have to accept that stepping out of the school realm in this way can mean anything from success to summer school to failing the grade. If you aren't at the point where you are willing to let your child truly suffer the consequences for his behavior, plan B is not for you.

While plan B is difficult to follow through, from the vantage point of your child's future, it is much better to fail a class or even an entire grade and learn a lesson early than it is not to learn the lesson and end up not going to college, failing out of college, or being unable to manage his own life once school has ended. You will have to think plan B through before you commit to it, because if say you will let your child fail and then bail him out at the last minute, that will teach the very opposite of the lesson you intended to teach.

PLAN C: MICROMANAGEMENT

The only real way to create success where there's no desire for it is to demand performance. By demanding that all homework is complete and all tests are studied for, you are showing your child that he is, in fact, capable of succeeding, but that she has not yet learned that success comes only through ongoing effort. This means that you will have to step into your child's academics in a very aggressive and consistent manner.

You will have to insist that every assignment be written down in an agenda and every book brought home every day. You will have to create a significant penalty when these things do not occur. You will need to set up both a time and a place for studying, and you will have to inspect the work to find out if it is completed and placed in a spot where it can be turned in the next day. You will have to insist that as homework assignments are completed, they are checked off in the agenda and then crossed through after they have been turned in. This creates a visual reminder for your child throughout the day that completed work is being handed in and provides a record for you at the end of each school day that your child has followed through with your instructions. This means you will have to stay in tune to the requirements of each class by keeping up with the teachers' blogs or by emailing them regularly to confirm that work is being turned in on time.

Finally, you will have to become an expert at overcoming your child's objections and misdirections. The following is a chart that can help you reinterpret your child's comments and respond in a way that keeps the ball in your court. After the chart are some additional tools to help you manage your child's course load.

Understanding your child's "school speak"

What your child says	What it usually means	How you can respond	Result
"I don't have any homework"	There is no physical sheet of paper that I have to write on and turn back in tomorrow.	What else is going on in the class? IS there a test, quiz or project we can start on?	Your child spends time reviewing notes from class today and learns that there is a difference between what is due and what needs to be done.
"I forgot it"	I don't want to do it.	Ok. Let me find something similar for you to practice on the internet, so you don't fall behind in those skills	You call your child's bluff and teach him/her that "forgetting" work doesn't mean that you don't have to do any work.. in fact it may have been easier to have brought the assignment home than to have done the harder one you came up with.
"It isn't due for a long time"	"I don't know how or don't want to start on it now.	Let's look at it together and just make a plan for what needs to be done.	Teaches long term planning. Relieves the fear of starting and the feeling of being overwhelmed by the size of the project.
"We haven't learned that yet"	"I don't know how or don't want to start on it now.	Let's look at it together and introduce the concept so when your teacher does it you will already have a headstart.	Teaches that the child can learn things in advance and experience greater confidence during the actual lesson.
"That is not how my teacher showed us"	I don't understand how to do this and listening to you say it in a new way is frustrating.	Show me how your teacher explained it and I will help you understand what she said.	Teaches that there is more than one way to get a right answer and that it is helpful to talk through what you are trying to understand.

Day_____   **Date:** _____

Complete this checklist with your child every day after school.

I. Planner (15 minutes)

_____ **Yesterday's plan:** HW crossed off Y____N____ HW has been turned in Y____N____

_____ **Homework today:** Discuss each subject: Math, Spanish/French, Social Studies/History, Language Arts/ Literature, Science, other_____

_____ Is it written in planner? **Notes:**_____

_____ Has it been checked off? **Notes:**_____

_____ Is it filed in correct place? **Notes:**_____

_____ **Tests/quizzes coming up**

_____ Write a study plan (in the planner) for each day prior to the test/quiz.

_____ **Daily study: Choose and** complete specific tasks in each subject

(Limit daily studying for tests/quizzes to thirty minutes and work on it daily.)

_____ **Long-term projects**

_____ Create a daily checklist for completing the project in twenty minutes a day.

Notes: _____

_____

_____

II. Backpack (5–10 minutes)

Take a look at miscellaneous papers. Check inside books too.

_____ Have your child file papers in the folders where they belong.

Notes:_____

_____

_____

III. Work completion

Your child can use the remaining time to complete any homework, tests, quizzes, or projects. First choose anything that he may need help with, then allow him to work independently on the rest. Follow up at the end to see that the work is packed up and ready to be turned in the next day. Make notes that explain what work he did and what work he needed help on.

_____

_____

_____

_____

_____

_____

_____

_____

_____

_____

Homework vs. study time

Homework is a stated school expectation. *If you just meet the expectation, you should expect a C in the class.*

Studying is an implied school expectation. *If you study on a regular basis, you are going beyond the basic expectation of simply completing assignments. This is how you will raise your grade to a B or an A.*

These tasks are to be done *in addition to* the homework for each of these subjects. (See the daily checklist to make sure you don't forget any homework assignments.)

For each of the subjects you are taking in school, complete at least one task each night. The chapters in this book explain specific tasks in each subject area.

Use the checklist below to write down which tasks you have completed in each subject. Include the chapter and section number that the task was applied to.

SUBJECT	Mon	Tue	Wed	Thu	Fri	Sat	Sun
History							
Science							
Literature							
Spanish							
Math							

CHAPTER 9

TIME: WHY DO I HAVE LESS OF IT THAN OTHER PEOPLE?

First, let's make sure this is true. Other people have twenty-four hours in each day. How many do you have? Yes, I am just kidding to make a point, which is this: it's not how many hours you have that's the problem; it's how you have chosen to spend those hours. Time management is really a simple issue of priorities. Before you continue reading, fill out every half hour of the chart below with your activities during the day.

Weekly Schedule

	Monday	Tuesday	Wednesday	Thursday	Friday	Saturday	Sunday
3:30 - 4:00							
4:00 - 4:30							
4:30 - 5:00							
5:00 - 5:30							
5:30 - 6:00							
6:00 - 6:30							
6:30 - 7:00							
7:00 - 7:30							
7:30 - 8:00							
8:00 - 8:30							
8:30 - 9:30							
9:30 - 10:30							

Use your chart to answer the questions below.

How much free time do you have?_____

How much time is devoted to extracurricular activities (such as dance, music, sports)? _____

How much time do you spend "hanging out" with your family (dinner, TV, chatting)? _____

How much time do you spend on homework and studying? _____

Because we spend time doing the things that are important to us, answering these questions should have made the things you care about more obvious. It should also have highlighted the areas that you can steal time from so you can spend more time on the things you care about. That is where the change will need to occur if you hope to improve your grades.

TIME TO CHANGE

FIRST, make a list of each subject you take in school, and calculate how much time it takes to complete homework in each class.

SECOND, add to that homework time at least twenty minutes of nightly studying, because what everyone in your life has told you is true: you must review a little bit at a time to guarantee success. That is a fact, so accept it and add the time.

THIRD, rework your weekly schedule to account for the amount of time you *actually* need for success in school. You will find a chart on the next page that will allow you to write out your "New Weekly Schedule".

FINALLY, make a commitment to spend this time focused on school work. Use the previous chapters in this book to make that time effective and productive and watch those grades improve!

NFWII Weekly Schedule

	Monday	Tuesday	Wednesday	Thursday	Friday	Saturday	Sunday
3:30 - 4:00							
4:00 - 4:30							
4:30 - 5:00							
5:00 - 5:30							
5:30 - 6:00							
6:00 - 6:30							
6:30 – 7:00							
7:00 – 7:30							
7:30 – 8:00							
8:00 - 8:30							
8:30 - 9:30							
9:30 - 10:30							

Parent Perspective: Is Your Child Really Too Busy?

Once I worked with a student I'll call Jimmy who had a fifty-seven in his English class because he read two years below his grade level. We worked with him for a few months, and then his mother called. She was concerned that Jimmy seemed "too stressed over everything he has to do." She felt that she needed to drop the tutoring to create some downtime for Jimmy. Her claim was that he "didn't have any time that was just for him."

Concerned, and a bit curious, I asked about Jimmy's schedule of activities, and this is what I learned: Jimmy played baseball three nights a week from five until seven-thirty. He had private batting lesson on another night. One night each week he went to his church youth group, and he had just been asked to join a lacrosse team at the YMCA, which met twice a week.

The mother was right that Jimmy didn't have time to continue the tutoring if he added the lacrosse, but the fact that Jimmy didn't have any time "just for himself" was totally false. *All* his time was for himself! Every activity was a choice about how he spent his time. His mother's idea of cutting out tutoring so he could have some time to sit down sent the message to Jimmy that academics are the least important thing in his life; second, even, to doing nothing at all!

There is no doubt that we all need downtime, but if your child uses that time to join a sport, you can't allow him to cut time out of schoolwork, sleep, or eating well to create more free time. Imagine the consequences if (since you are so busy with activities on the weekend) you took a day off each week from your job so you could have some time to yourself.

As adults, we've learned that we must do what is required of us before we get to do what entertains us. We work first, and we play when we are finished. Don't be afraid to teach your child the same lesson.

As the parent, it is up to you to make it clear to your children—from the beginning—how much time is theirs to enjoy (by doing nothing or joining something) and how much time will be devoted to schoolwork. Teaching them that school is a priority with your words and your actions will help them manage their time much better.

summary

In an effort to tie the ideas presented in this book together (without a lengthy restatement of the book itself) I have made an acronym of the key points made in the previous chapters. Some of these can serve as a mantra for you; statements you repeat to yourself as a reminder to keep yourself focused on the task at hand. Find one or two that speak to you and copy them into your agenda to serve as a reminder of what you are choosing to do as a student. And always remember: "If you want to, you can!"

Interest in the material is not a requirement for success.
For success you simply need a willingness to do the work.

You will focus better with less distraction.
Off with the electronics while you study.
Understanding the material lasts longer than memorizing it.

Waiting to the last minute guarantees lower quality work.
Active participation in class builds interest.
Needing to study is totally normal.
Training is required for success to occur.

Taking your time pays off.
Organization is not a gift you get, it is a skill you build.

You will continue to make excuses until you accept the responsibility.
Other people cannot succeed for you.
Underneath it all, you know you want success.

Continual effort produces results.
Accepting responsibility builds character.
Needing help is not unusual.

Proof

23226295R10072

Made in the USA
Charleston, SC
15 October 2013